COOL CAREERS WITHOUT COLLEGE FOR
MUSIC
LOVERS

COOL CAREERS WITHOUT COLLEGE FOR
MUSIC
LOVERS

**KERRY
HINTON**

The Rosen Publishing Group, Inc.
New York

Published in 2002 by The Rosen Publishing Group, Inc.
29 East 21st Street, New York, NY 10010

First Edition

Library of Congress Cataloging-in-Publication Data

Hinton, Kerry.
Cool careers without college for music lovers / Kerry Hinton.— 1st ed.
p. cm. — (Cool careers without college)
Includes lists of Web sites, bibliographical references, and index.
ISBN 0-8239-3503-5 (library binding)
1. Music—Vocational guidance—Juvenile literature. [1. Music—
Vocational guidance. 2. Vocational guidance.] I. Title. II. Series.
ML3795 .H64 2002
780'.23'73—dc21

2001004184

Manufactured in the United States of America

CONTENTS

INTRODUCTION

Do you love music? If your answer is yes, then keep reading! This book is all about music. It's not about the latest hit song or newest video, it's a more practical look at music—how to include it in what you choose as a possible career.

None of the jobs that you will find listed in this book require a college degree, but they all demand what most jobs do to ensure success: dedication and patience. You do not even need to know how to play a musical instrument for the majority of these jobs!

This book contains twelve different professions that are associated with music in various ways. Each chapter describes a job, the training you may need, and places where you can find out more information. Many of the jobs can be combined with one another or can be accomplished while you work at more "traditional" jobs. Maybe you haven't even considered some of them. Who knows? This book may give you an idea for an exciting future you might not have thought of before now!

1

RETAIL STORE EMPLOYEE

Record and CD stores are essential to the music industry. They provide record companies with places to put their products so that consumers can buy them. The great thing about working in record stores is the access you can have—not only to great music, but also to great contacts in the music industry for future jobs. Many people who

Getting a job as a salesperson in a record store can be a great way to break into the music business.

work in various levels and segments of the music industry today started in retail, either managing or working in a store and gaining valuable knowledge and experience before moving to another field connected to music.

Description

Job responsibilities vary from store to store. For example, at a large chain outlet you may only have one job, like doing stock and inventory or running a register station. Smaller mom and pop stores traditionally have fewer employees on their staffs, so you may get a chance to do and see more at an earlier stage there. Music stores are great places to learn about music, which is crucial to other jobs concerning music in this book.

In addition to hearing all kinds of music, you can gain insight into the workings of the music industry. You can also have the chance to meet and talk with representatives from record labels and promotion companies, who often may have leads to entry-level employment opportunities at record labels, distribution companies, or other music-related jobs.

The next step up in music retail usually includes additional duties, such as buying. If you enjoy music, this part should be very appealing. As a buyer, you have a budget determined either by you, the owner, or the manager of the particular store. You are free to use this budget toward purchasing a product. Depending on the store, this could expand to include a variety of items, such as compact discs, vinyl records, Walkmans, guitar strings, music magazines, blank tapes, videos, and other music accessories. Large and independent record labels will contact you on a daily basis to keep you informed of all of the most recent and up-to-the-minute happenings and releases. It's up to a buyer to look at a store's sales history and its buying customers to determine quantities of records that he or she will purchase for a particular establishment. Larger chain stores sometimes have one buyer for

Working in a music store gives you an opportunity to explore music that you may otherwise be unfamiliar with.

a particular style or type of music. For instance, you may be the jazz buyer for a store. If you don't know that much about jazz, this would be a great opportunity to expand your listening horizons, while at the same time becoming more knowledgeable and more valuable to a store or to another sector of the music industry.

Managing a store in one capacity or another is usually the final promotion people can receive at a retail outlet. Managers have more responsibility than do hourly wage employees; at smaller, more independent stores, managers

A record store employee checks out new music at one of the store's listening stations.

do the buying as well as managing the store, and can also be responsible for duties like scheduling work shifts, signing checks, and paying bills and employees.

Education and Training

No particular education is required. If you want to work at a retail outlet, simply apply for a job. Like other fields, store managers and owners look for people who are friendly, trustworthy, and dependable. Music stores need employees who have a good base of knowledge of music, and/or a real motivation to learn about it. Training is almost always on-the-job. Simply put, you learn as you go—by experience.

Salary

Like most retail jobs, record and CD stores usually start at a wage slightly higher than minimum wage. However, employee turnover is very high in retail, so employees who seek out additional responsibilities and show that they can be counted on have the best chance of moving up or receiving higher pay more quickly. At the managerial level, salaries vary by geographical location and the size of a particular business. In New York City, for example, a buyer or manager at a retail store could expect to start in the $25,000 per year range and move up annually.

Outlook

The outlook for a career as a retail store employee is above average. Although there are fewer local music stores than in previous years, there are many chain retail outlets that are always looking for employees. The Department of Labor predicts that retail jobs will increase by 14 percent over the next few years. In addition, there are now also many Internet-based music retailers who still need a workforce despite the lack of face-to-face interactions with customers.

Additional Information

The atmosphere in most retail stores can be very energizing, especially if you're excited about the product you are helping to promote or sell. The dress code at most stores is very informal, most likely very relaxed. Music is a leisure activity, and retail stores strive to create a shopping environment where people can be comfortable and enjoy themselves. Remember that ultimately you're offering service to the customer; on some level, you must enjoy working with people to succeed. Also, since you're working in retail, it is helpful to have a good mind for business and financial matters, as you'll be making cash and credit transactions and inventorying stock.

Profile

Ten Questions with Bronko Spaleta

Manager, Sam Goody, Hoboken, New Jersey

WHAT IS YOUR TITLE?
Store Manager.

HOW LONG HAVE YOU WORKED HERE?
I've been with the company for ten years, and at this location for one and a half years.

HOW DID YOU GET THIS JOB?
Quite by accident. I was a regular shopper at a nearby Sam Goody in the late 1980s. One day, the manager

asked me if I wanted a full-time cashier position. That's how it started!

DID YOU GO TO COLLEGE FOR THIS JOB?

No. I did go for media studies, but it doesn't really apply to my work here.

WHAT IS THE DOWNSIDE OF YOUR JOB?

Crazy hours! We work an uneven schedule with a lot of weekend shifts—it's our busiest time. It's also sometimes hard to manage employees who refuse to do their jobs even though they know their duties.

WHAT'S THE UPSIDE?

Free concert tickets, access to great music, and teamwork with fun employees who like music just as much as I do.

DO YOU HAVE MUCH RESPONSIBILITY?

Yes! I'm responsible for everything, even when I'm not here. If one of my employees is rude to a customer, he represents me. It's the same as my being rude to that customer. It's tough to motivate employees sometimes, too. I need their help to get work completed, even though I'm responsible for it.

DO YOU HAVE TO HIRE AND FIRE PEOPLE?

All the time. People leave for all reasons, and I couldn't tell you how many I've had to bring on board and let go over the years.

DO YOU LIKE YOUR JOB?

No.

NO?

No. I love it.

FOR MORE INFORMATION

ASSOCIATIONS

Music and Entertainment Industry Student Association (MEISA)
Web site: http://www.wiu.edu/users/mimusba/meisa
A global organization of students working with educators and music industry professionals to prepare for careers in music.

The Music Industries Association of Canada (MIAC)
33 Medhurst Road
Toronto, ON M4B 1B2
(416) 490-1871
e-mail: info@miac.net
Web site: http://www.miac.net
A national, nonprofit trade association representing Canadian manufacturers, wholesalers, distributors, and retailers of music-related products.

National Association of Music Merchants (NAMM)
5790 Armada Drive
Carlsbad, CA 92008
(800) 767-6266
Web site: http://www.namm.com
Everything you need to know about products for the music industry. Includes news, information about industry events, and online courses.

WEB SITES

Billboard.com
http://www.billboard.com
Online component of *Billboard* magazine, offering news, charts, trivia, and reviews.

Ice Magazine
http://www.icemagazine.com
Ice Magazine is a music store's friend. It's available as a print magazine also. Both the Web site and the magazine list news about all types of music. Most important, each features a comprehensive five- to eight-page monthly listing of upcoming releases and reissues.

Independent Retail Directory
http://www.the-ird.com
An extensive online database that catalogs the best and brightest of U.S. indie record stores, and can even steer you to the best near you.

Internet Music Resource Guide
http://www.specialweb.com/music
A reference of links and other resources to Internet sites about music.

Play de Record
http://209.20.29.40/wax.html
An interesting Web site that tells the story of a music fan who decided to try his hand at running his own store. This site is good if opening a business is your goal.

PERIODICALS

Alternative Press
Web site: http://www.altpress.com
Features reviews, news, and features for fans of alternative, indie, ska, electronic, dub, industrial, punk, techno, underground, rock, ambient, and experimental music.

Canadian Music Trade
Web site: http://www.canadianmusictrade.com
A publication serving Canadian music dealers and suppliers.

The Gavin Report
140 Second Street
5th Floor
San Francisco, CA 94105
(415) 495-1990
Web site: http://www.gavin.com
This print trade journal, along with its online component, covers the American radio industry. It also collects and compiles playlists of more than 1,300 radio stations.

Jelly
Web site: http://www.jellyroll.com
Reviews of blues, jazz, country, soul, and rock.

Mojo
Web site: http://www.mojo4music.com
A British music magazine with intelligent writing focusing on rock music.

Music Business
Web site: http://www.musicbusiness.co.uk
The leading monthly trade magazine for musical instrument retailers, distributors, manufacturers, and recording studios.

Pollstar
4697 W. Jacquelyn Avenue
Fresno, CA 93722
(559) 271-7900
Web site: http://www.pollstar.com
A print magazine with an online component, *Pollstar* publishes concert tour schedules for music professionals.

Rolling Stone
Web site: http://www.rollingstone.com
A monthly popular culture magazine covering the entertainment industry with a special focus on music.

Spin
Web site: http://www.spin.com
The print and online versions of this magazine cover everything you'd want to know about the latest in rock music.

FOR FUN

Hornby, Nick. *High Fidelity.* New York: Riverhead Books, 1995.
A novel about the culture of music fanatics and the record store environment. It is also a movie starring John Cusack.

Empire Records (1995)
Warner Bros.
A movie about a day in the life of young record store employees, starring Liv Tyler.

2

PROFESSIONAL DJ

Playing music for the general public is not just reserved for radio personalities anymore. If you have a good-sized collection of records or compact discs, you may want to try your hand at playing music for income. No matter what the name or how it happens to be spelled—DeeJay, DJ, Disc Jockey—this is yet another way to make music part of your employment future.

Description

Depending on the type of music and venue you are interested in, the setting of your job may vary. Performing as a DJ can take you from spinning records at local events like parties all the way to traveling and playing music for hundreds or even thousands of people. Some DJs only perform to supplement their incomes; some work so often that they need managers and booking agents to keep track of their busy schedules. Both ends of the spectrum can be entertaining, rewarding, and lucrative.

The first step to becoming a DJ is to obtain equipment. Depending on how much equipment you need, prices may vary. You may not want to spend a large amount of money in the early stages, at least until you decide whether or not deejaying is for you. The main tool of any DJ is a set of two devices that can play music—they can be two turntables, two CD players, or another combination. They need to be portable, because at larger venues, DJs are usually expected to arrive with their own equipment and to connect it to a sound system provided by the establishment that hires them. You'll also need some sort of a mixer.

A disc jockey spins records at a backyard party.

A mixer is crucial to playing music on records or CDs for an audience because it allows you to shift from turntable to turntable or CD player to CD player to "mix" the music so it can be heard without any gaps, stops, or interruptions. Some CD players on the market have a mixer built in, and you can often find package deals on the market that combine a mixer with a player.

Once you have the basic equipment, the next step is to make a tape. Doing this is very important. A mixed tape is basically your audio résumé—it will let people who are considering hiring you hear what you have to offer as a DJ. Make sure the tape isn't too long and that it presents a good sample of your musical range; remember, DJs with more musical knowledge (which equals variety in musical selections) have a better chance of securing gigs. Once you have a tape that represents your abilities, you'll need to shop it around. Pounding the pavement is an important aspect of the profession. You can accomplish this by mailing copies to people who regularly look for DJs, like promoters, club owners, and club managers.

One type of DJ is the club DJ. Club DJs play their music at parties, local clubs, and other events. If things go well (meaning people come to hear you and want to keep coming back) you may be rewarded with a residency. In short, a residency is a regular performance slot on a regular basis.

Residencies are usually weekly or monthly, and they are good goals to reach for.

Another way to earn money as a DJ is by performing at specialty events such as weddings, birthday parties, and other sorts of celebrations. In this case, you'll still need a tape or some kind of sampling of your playlist. You also need to be flexible, because people who hold and schedule these events usually have a more specific idea of what they would like their guests to hear. Obviously, most people do not get married repeatedly in their lives, and birthdays only come once a year, so the concept of a residency doesn't really apply here. However, events like these are good opportunities to promote yourself; you could find yourself performing for many of the guests at their birthdays or weddings.

One initial drawback to deejaying may be age. Many places that hire DJs also serve alcohol and, depending on the state, may have restrictions regarding employing people under the legal drinking age. However, there are still plenty of places to play besides clubs of this sort, such as school dances, corporate events, and family gatherings.

Education and Training

No formal training is necessary once you purchase equipment, but practice is. Before a hopeful DJ makes a tape to

High school functions, such as proms and concerts, are likely sources of work for disc jockeys.

shop around, he or she has to know the ins and outs of the equipment. There are a few videos out there that can teach you the basics, or you can ask a friend who has some experience to show them to you. Once you've got them down, you can have fun developing your own style. This is one field in which individuality can really make a difference.

Salary

Pay varies for DJs. If you manage to play a considerable amount and make a name for yourself, you can request more money than a DJ who is just starting out. Pay is usually on a per-night basis and is influenced by many factors, including venue size and attendance. One way to find a basic amount to charge would be to contact other DJs in your area and ask them what they charge.

Outlook

The outlook for deejaying seems to be very good. DJ culture is very popular at the moment. Many establishments hire people to play music for a more personal touch these days, and people who host events look for DJs who can help to make their celebrations or gatherings as enjoyable and memorable as possible.

FOR MORE INFORMATION

ASSOCIATIONS

American Disc Jockey Association
1964 Wagner Street
Pasadena, CA 91107
(626) 844-3204
Web site: http://www.adja.org
This professional organization supports disc jockeys, provides them with continuing education, and offers news about the industry.

Canadian Disc Jockey Association
336 Yonge Street, Suite 141
Barrie, ON L4N 4C8
(519) 453-3136
e-mail: heckendr@cdja.org
Web site: http://www.cdja.org
This is a nonprofit trade association for disc jockeys across Canada.

Online Disc Jockey Association (ODJA)
3600 Magnolia Avenue
Reading, PA 19605
(610) 929-4315
e-mail: odja@odja.com
Web site: http://www.odja.com
ODJA promotes professionalism and maintains the highest standards in the disc jockey industry. The ODJA provides members with discounted insurance, advertising, and much more.

WEB SITES
Dusty Groove Records
http://www.dustygroove.com
Dusty groove is an online merchant specializing in rare funky jazz, hip-hop, soul, and Latin music.

Groove Merchant Records
http://www.fogworld.com/gm
This is a great source for rare groove and hip-hop records.

Turntable Lab
http://www.turntablelab.com
This site is an online source for buying DJ equipment and goods.

BOOKS
Brewster, Bill, and Frank Broughton. *Last Night a DJ Saved My Life*. New York: Grove Press, 2000.

Written by two music journalists who interviewed professional DJs, music critics, industry insiders, and musicians, *Last Night a DJ Saved My Life* charts the history and examines the psychology of the disc jockey.

Lindquist, Robert A. *Spinnin' 2000: The Ultimate Guide to Fun and Profit as a Mobile DJ*. E. Rochester, NY: LA Communications, 1990. For the prospective DJ, a guide to making a living by playing music.

Poshardt, Ulf, and Shaun Whiteside. *Dj-Culture*. London: Quartet Books Ltd, 2000. Poshardt focuses on the DJ's role in music history from record spinner to musician.

Reighley, Kurt B. *Looking for the Perfect Beat: The Art and Culture of the DJ*. New York: Pocket Books, 2000. This book features interviews with real disc jockeys, chronicles the history of spinning, and also provides practical advice to the novice DJ.

Sabatke, Donald D. *Jock Itch: For Those Itching to Be a DJ*. Ixonia, WI: The Broadcasters Learning Center, 1997. This book offers solid advice on turntable techniques for the beginner disc jockey.

Webber, Stephen. *Turntable Technique: The Art of the DJ*. Milwaukee, WI: Hal Leonard Publishing Corporation, 2000. This is as close to a DJ textbook as you'll find. It comes with two albums to help the aspiring DJ learn how to match beats.

Zemon, Stacy. *The Mobile DJ Handbook: How to Start and Run a Profitable Mobile Disc Jockey Service*. Boston: Focal Press, 1997. This book contains valuable practical information on buying equipment, getting bookings and negotiating contracts, advertising, and other business-related tips and strategies.

PERIODICALS

Dance Music Authority (DMA)
Web site: http://www.dmadance.com
This online magazine offers features, interviews, and news about house music and the DJ scene.

DJ Times
Web site: http://www.djtimes.com
DJ Times is a trade magazine for professional DJs. This site features video interviews with top DJs, information about the industry, charts, news, and more.

DJzone
Web site: http://www.djzone.net
DJzone is the largest online network for disc jockeys. It includes articles, resources, and business advice for the professional DJ.

Mobile Beat: The DJ Magazine
Web site: http://www.mobilebeat.com
Mobile Beat is dedicated to the specialized interests of working mobile entertainers. Each issue is packed with coverage and reviews of new equipment and music along with tips on how to boost bookings and get more referrals from each performance.

The Wire
Web site: http://www.thewire.co.uk
The Wire is a monthly magazine focusing on electronica, avant rock, breakbeat jazz, modern classical, and global music.

XLR8R (pronounced "accelerator")
Web site: http://www.xlr8r.com
This monthly magazine covers electronic music and rave culture.

VIDEOS

(All available from DMC USA, 213 West 35th Street, #402, New York, NY 10001)

The Art of Turntablism
The world's greatest DJs teach techniques.

Shure Turntablism 101
This video focuses on the philosophy of the DJ, going beyond techniques to provide the thoughts that go with the maneuvers. An all-star lineup of professional DJs break down their routines and explain the philosophy behind their moves.

So You Wanna Be a DJ?
Techniques, explanations of studio technology, and interviews with top radio DJs and programmers.

3

RECORD DISTRIBUTION COMPANY EMPLOYEE

Record companies deal with what everyone wants to hear: music. In some ways, record companies form the center of the music industry as we know it today. Recorded sound accounts for a great deal of employment opportunities. Record companies are responsible for the recording, promotion, and supply of various projects from a variety of musicians and singers. There are dozens and dozens of jobs in this field—some record companies occupy two or three floors of a large office building! We'll focus on the positions that you're more likely to obtain soon after graduating high school.

Description

Every person who works at a record distribution company is very important to the end goal—getting music to the general public—and positions are usually available at lower levels. The lowest of these involves working on what is called a street team.

Street teams are assembled by employees of a record company to perform a series of special tasks that the record company employees may not be able to perform. These tasks may include hanging posters, handing out flyers and stickers, or checking on quantities of specific records at various stores in a certain area. Street team jobs are part-time and primarily intended for high-school and college students. There are other jobs within record companies, and many of them are intern positions. As with other jobs, you may not get paid immediately, but they are good stepping-stones to jobs that do pay.

Working on a street team or as an intern will make you familiar to more than a few people at a record company; this is important if a paid position opens up. The entry-level

A record company's mailroom is an excellent entry point into the music business. There, a young person comes into contact with managers from various departments who can help advance his or her career.

positions at record companies literally start at the bottom—in the basement! That's usually where the mailroom is.

The mailroom is very important to the running of a record company; regular mail is still the best way to ensure that record stores and people who are going to buy records know about upcoming releases, titles they may have missed hearing, and special offers a record company may be offering to the buying public. Working in the mailroom can be a good place to be since members of various departments in a record company spend a good part of their days traveling to the mailroom. What does this mean? This is an excellent way to become known and to meet people in the company. Many record company promotions come from within. Also, since mailroom employees are really at the heart of the company, they get to see how all departments operate. If you know you want to work for a record company, but you're unsure about what you actually want to do, this can give you a taste of different jobs before committing to them.

From the mailroom, it's all uphill. A logical next step would be the job of merchandising coordinator, which involves doing everything needed to get the posters and flyers and checklists to the street teams. Merchandising coordinators are given a small budget by their superiors to complete these tasks, and it is often very challenging to do so.

Merchandising coordinators report to product development representatives (PDRs). PDRs may be placed in charge of a certain record or an artist, and it's their job to publicize a record so that people will buy it. PDRs may work on one record or artist at a time, concentrating only on that project. At other times, PDRs may have ten priorities to divide their time among, which is usually the case.

Education and Training

No formal education is necessary. Out of all of the professions in this guide, the recording industry probably has the largest number of employees who did not go to college to train for their jobs. Colleges don't offer record company degrees, which helps to make the playing field more even. Hard work is very important once you get your foot in the door in the record industry. Individuals who volunteer for tough assignments or harder jobs with longer hours are the employees who learn more at a quicker rate. They are also the ones who are easier to remember when promotion time rolls around. Be motivated! It does help, as we've mentioned before, to know a lot about music, which is why many record store employees switch fields and find work at record companies.

Salary

Salary depends on the specific job. A person who works on a street team usually will not get paid, but some companies do offer anywhere from the state minimum wage to $10 an hour to individuals who hang posters or hand out flyers to advertise a record label's product. Mailroom salaries are low and can often start at around $18,000 a year. By the time a person is a PDR, he or she may make around

This audience at the Concert for the Rock and Roll Hall of Fame in Cleveland, Ohio, is likely to have included record company employees who got free tickets at work.

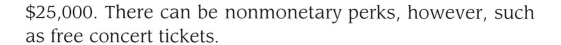

$25,000. There can be nonmonetary perks, however, such as free concert tickets.

Outlook

There is a high amount of turnover at record companies, especially in lower-level positions. If one company doesn't have a need for interns, keep looking—odds are there is work to be found. As with other jobs involving music, you may want to combine your work at a record company with another job until you begin to move up in the ranks.

Additional Information

Start small. The smaller the company, the fewer employees there are. This means that it will be easier to be known around the office and to receive more responsibility at an earlier point in your career. You should also be hopeful, yet realistic. Understand that it may be a long time before you are out on the road, scouting out small towns for the next big band, so be patient.

Record companies are open during the day, but musicians mostly play at night. If you think that working with record labels and artists is for you, remember that it involves working during the day and also during some of your off time. You may have to attend a concert to help ensure that a band's show runs smoothly. You may have to stay later than normal to get a large mailing together or to work on a flyer to distribute to street teams. The music industry is a busy one, especially when you work at a record company. Be prepared to throw away your idea of a traditional nine-to-five schedule.

Also remember that the music business is always changing. If you can think of a job that hasn't been created yet, invent it yourself! Innovation is one of the hallmarks of the business.

FOR MORE INFORMATION

ASSOCIATIONS

Creative Musicians Coalition
1-24 W. Willcox Avenue
Peoria, IL 61604
(309) 685-4843
e-mail: info@amimcmc.com
Web site: http://www.aimcmc.com
This is an international organization dedicated to the advancement of new music and the success of the independent musician.

Taxi

Web site: http://www.taxi.com

(800) 458-2111

This is an independent artist and repertoire company helping unsigned bands, artists, and songwriters get deals and promotions. It is also helpful for industry listings.

WEB SITES

BMG Entertainment

http://www.bmgentertainment.com

BMG is one of the largest distributors worldwide. They represent hundreds of artists and operate all over the globe.

Independent Record Distribution Network

http://www.pan.com/indie/dist.htm

This is an online resource for distributing audio recordings that have been independently produced and released.

Internet Music Resource Guide

http://www.specialweb.com/music

This site is a reference of links and other resources to Internet sites about music.

Revolver USA

http://www.midheaven.com/revolverusa/links.html

Revolver is an independent music distributor that carries some well-known and lesser-known artists. Its eclectic roster is worth checking out, as are the FAQs about the company.

Soundclick.com

http://www.soundclick.com

This site features signed and unsigned bands. Labels can send MP3s of their artists to the site.

Studio K7

http://www.k7.com

Studio K7 is a fast-rising music distributor that deals mainly with electronic music. The Web site also looks cool.

BOOKS

Frascogna, Xavier M., and H. Lee Hetherington. *This Business of Artist Management.* New York: Billboard Books, 1997.
This Business of Artist Management will help anyone intending to work with musicians for a living.

Kashif and Gary Greenberg. *Everything You'd Better Know About the Record Industry*. Venice, CA: Brooklyn Boy Books, 1996.
This book is a comprehensive guide for anyone who wants to pursue a career in the music industry. Rapper Ice Cube calls it the new bible for the recording industry.

Krasilovsky, M. William, Sidney Shemel, and John Gross. *This Business of Music: The Definitive Guide to the Music Industry*. New York: Watson-Guptill Publishers, 2000.
This is a comprehensive reference to the economic, legal, and financial aspects of the music business. It is known as the definitive book on the music industry.

Lathrop, Tad, and Jim Pettigrew. *This Business of Music Marketing and Promotion*. New York: Billboard Books, 1999.
This is a guide to planning and producing a complete marketing campaign for selling music to the listening public.

Passman, Donald S. *All You Need to Know About the Music Busines*s. New York: Simon and Schuster, 2000.
This book gives advice about negotiating deals, advisers, publishing, touring, and merchandising. It includes helpful information for anyone interested in pursuing a career in the music industry.

Schwartz, Daylle Deanna. *Start and Run Your Own Record Label*. New York: Billboard Books, 1998.
This is specially good for beginners. Quotes from industry professionals will help those who need to know all aspects of the music business.

Sweeney, Tim, and Mark Geller. *Tim Sweeney's Guide to Releasing Independent Records*. Torrance, CA: T.S.A. Books, 1996.
This book teaches the reader how to set up his or her own independent label, produce records, get distribution into major retail outlets, design a promotional strategy, and get records played.

PERIODICALS

Billboard
1515 Broadway
New York, NY 10036
(212) 764-7300
Web site: http://www.billboard.com
Billboard is a very well-known weekly magazine dealing with the music industry. It covers all bases, such as independent music and world music. A good place to find out who the movers and shakers are in the industry. It is available at libraries and newsstands.

The Gavin Report
140 Second Street, 5th Floor
San Francisco, CA 94105
(415) 495-1990
Web site: http://www.gavin.com
This print trade journal, along with its online component, covers the American radio industry. It also collects and compiles playlists of more than 1,300 radio stations.

Pollstar
4697 W. Jacquelyn Avenue
Fresno, CA 93722
(559) 271-7900
Web site: http://www.pollstar.com
A print magazine with an online component, *Pollstar* publishes concert tour schedules for music professionals.

4

AUDIO ENGINEER

Audio engineers (also called sound technicians) can perform a wide range of jobs. They deal with the processing of live and recorded sound, which covers a large number of employment possibilities and can also lead to other related job opportunities in the music industry.

An audio engineer uses a mixing board to test audio levels before a live performance.

Description

Simply put, audio engineers make things sound good. Audio engineers process sound; that is, they work with sound that comes through microphones, amplifiers, or other sources, and they adjust the levels of the various sounds (the bass, drums, voice, and guitar of a band, for instance) to make them work together as a whole listening experience. Audio engineers are often called soundmen or soundwomen, because sound is the focal point of their field.

Audio engineers adjust the sounds of live and recorded performances to ensure that everyone can hear what's being said or played and that the sound is as free of disturbances as possible. Disturbances refer to anything that interferes with sound quality. One good example is feedback, which is the high-pitched sound that you may hear when someone talks into a microphone. Audio engineers also think about how sound will travel in a particular place, and they know exactly where to put microphones or equipment to ensure maximum sound quality. If you look on the back of a CD or an album, the person who is credited as the "engineer" is actually an audio engineer. The producers of recorded music—CDs and records—often have audio engineer training as well.

A tool many audio engineers work with is called a mixing board, which is a more advanced version of the mixer that a DJ at a small to midsized event may use. Almost any public event—political speeches, television broadcasts, live concerts—requires the services of an audio engineer.

Audio engineers are also able to perform a great number of sound-related jobs. In addition to figuring out and monitoring sound requirements, they can also repair and service sound equipment. This can range from microphones to turntables to public address systems. Some areas of the

field involve the installation of sound systems at local clubs, arenas, and radio stations. Some sound technicians work in motion pictures and commercials, inserting necessary sound effects to enhance a program.

For larger or more complicated jobs, audio engineers often have assistants who help them with some of the details of a job. For instance, checking cables and connections for the sound at a stadium would be too much for one person to keep track of. Some people who have trained as audio engineers may start out helping someone in a very specific manner on their way to greater responsibilities.

Education and Training

Both education and training are necessary to be an effective and employable audio engineer. Some colleges offer sound engineering programs and classes; however, a college degree is not necessary to be an audio engineer. There are a few different pipelines to success or qualification. Check out the directory at the end of this chapter for associations that can tell you more about education opportunities in the field.

Audio engineers often take on jobs that are not directly music related. Here, members of an audio crew pack up cables for sound equipment they used for a political rally in Nashville.

Salary

Many soundmen and soundwomen who work at clubs and venues are paid on a per-night basis, and can use this experience to obtain a full-time job as an audio engineer on television or radio, where the median starting salary is about $18,000. With time in the business and more responsibility, audio engineers at very high levels can demand salaries upwards of $80,000 to $100,000.

Outlook

The outlook for audio engineers is good, thanks to the fact that there are many segments of the entertainment industry that rely on sound technicians. Freelance work can also be a good way to make steady or extra income; fill-in work for last-minute replacements can be in high demand. In addition to working with music, someone with an audio engineering background will be able to find work in a variety of connected fields such as special audio effects for motion pictures and music video sound.

Additional Information

Audio engineers frequently work long hours. The person in charge of sound for a concert can't arrive with the audience; he or she has to be at the venue hours earlier to

An audio engineer uses special equipment to test the sound system at an IMAX theater in Syracuse, New York.

check sound levels for various equipment. Many events that involve audio often take place at night or outside; this enables people in this field to work second jobs or to pursue other employment interests.

The field of audio engineering relies more and more on technology; an ability to understand computers or a willingness to learn is a great help. Lastly, audio engineers are in the spotlight, especially if there is a sound problem, which can occasionally make for a stressful environment.

Mixing Consoles

A mixing console, or mixing board, is the most important tool used by audio engineers. Indoors and out, mixing

boards allow the audience to hear a proper balance of all of the performers. Every microphone used in a performance is plugged in to the sound person's console. The board is really like a sound laboratory; all voices and sounds come together and are processed by the mixing board (this is what "mixing" is). Every mixing board has a series of channels, which allow the focus to be placed on different aspects of a performance.

A soundman monitors the balance of sounds at his mixing console.

Let's say a mixing board has sixteen channels. One of those channels may be devoted just to the bass guitar. This allows an audio engineer to adjust the bass guitar's level before it goes to the speaker. The engineer can prevent it from being too loud and drowning out other instruments, or from being too quiet and unheard by an audience. Imagine fifteen more items filling the remaining channels—that's the raw material of the soundperson's job during a performance. Using a mixing board allows sound personnel to adjust bass, treble, and midrange, and also to use electronic effects to enhance specific aspects of a performance, while allowing the rest of the band or orchestra to play on.

FOR MORE INFORMATION

ASSOCIATIONS

Audio Engineering Society (AES)
60 East 42nd Street, Room 2520
New York, NY 10165-2520
(212) 661-8528
e-mail: HQ@aes.org
Web site: http://www.aes.org

The AES is the only professional society devoted exclusively to audio technology. It serves its members, the industry, and the public by stimulating and facilitating advances in the constantly changing field of audio.

Recording Industry Association of America (RIAA)
1330 Connecticut Avenue NW
Suite 300
Washington, DC 20036
(202) 775-0101
Web site: http://www.riaa.com
A trade organization representing the U.S. recording industry.

WEB SITES

Modern Recording
http://www.modernrecording.com
Industry professionals share their expertise.

Prosound News
http://www.prosoundnews.com
This site has the latest on happenings and technology in the music sound industry.

ProSoundweb.com
http://www.live-audio.com
The Live Audio Board at www.live-audio.com has plenty of audio engineer resources.

The Recording Web Site
http://www.recordingwebsite.com
This site allows the user to make original music, get recording information and advice for a professional or home studio, and learn about audio production.

BOOKS

Massey, Howard. *Behind the Glass: Top Record Producers Tell How They Craft the Hits*. San Francisco, CA: Miller Freeman, 2000.
This book gives overviews of the creative and technical process of sound recording.

Owsinski, Bobby. *The Mastering Engineer's Handbook*. Vallejo, CA: Mix Books, 2000.
Interviews with professionals let the reader understand what the job is really about.

Owsinski, Bobby. *The Mixing Engineer's Handbook*. Emeryville, CA: Mix Books, 1999.
Points out the key elements of mixing for beginners.

Talbot-Smith, Michael. *Audio Engineer's Reference Book*. Boston: Focal Press, 1999.
Now in its second edition, this book reflects the latest technologies in sound engineering.

White, Ira. *Audio Made Easy: (Or How to Be a Sound Engineer Without Really Trying)*. Milwaukee, WI: Hal Leonard Publishing Corporation, 1997.
This book is an introduction to live audio and recording written by a professional audio engineer who is able to relate to the layman.

PERIODICALS

Audio Media
Web site: http://www.audiomedia.com
Audio Media bills itself as the world's leading professional audio technolgy magazine.

EQ
Web site: http://www.eqmag.com
EQ is a trade journal for serious recording professionals.

Home Recording
Web site: http://www.homerecordingmag.com
Home Recording caters to those who have home studios.

Mix
Web site:
http://industryclick.com/magazine.asp?magazineid=141&siteid=15
Mix is a trade magazine for those interested in commercial and project studio recording.

Professional Sound
Web site: http://www.professional-sound.com
This is a bimonthly trade journal for the professional sound engineer.

Studio Sound
Web site: http://www.studio-sound.com
This is a visually stunning trade journal that presents technical, high-end professional audio business information.

Tape Op
Web site: http://www.tapeop.com
This is the definitive journal of the music recording industry.

EDUCATIONAL PROGRAMS

Institute of Audio Research
64 University Place
New York, NY 10003
(212) 777-8550
Web site: http://www.audioschool.com
Located in New York City, the 600-hour Recording Engineering and Production (REP) Program offers both the in-depth technical knowledge and hands-on skills needed to begin a career in the recording industry as an assistant recording engineer or an entry-level audio technician.

Omega Recording Studios
5609 Fishers Lane
Rockville, MD 20852
(301) 230-9100
e-mail: omega@omegastudios.com
Web site: http://www.omegastudios.com
This program strives to prepare its students for the real world through instruction in the operation of recording studio, audio production, and sound reinforcement equipment. In addition, a music business curriculum is offered with the objective of preparing students for careers in the field of artist management.

The Recording Connection
(800) 295-4433
Web site: http://www.recordingconnection.com
A flexible, home-study program that provides students with hands-on training in music internships in their hometowns.

5

PROFESSIONAL MUSICIAN

As the name suggests, playing music can be a profession you pursue. There are important factors to consider, however, and we'll look at some of them over the next few pages. If you don't know how to play an instrument or how to sing, then this may not be the profession for you. Years of practice and dedication are necessary before a person can perform at the level of a professional musician.

Description

If you play an instrument, your services will probably fall into one of two categories: session musician or general business musician. Session musicians (also called session players, sidemen and sidewomen, or backup musicians) work in studios or onstage and are given a piece of music to learn and play according to the instructions of the band leader or producer of a recording session or concert. Session musicians are highly skilled and need to know how to read music and most likely write or transcribe music notation, which is the written language used by musicians everywhere.

Most session musicians specialize in one instrument or one type of instrument, such as stringed instruments or woodwinds, but playing more than one instrument can make you more valuable and can enable you to find work more often. Many session musicians don't perform onstage; they play their instruments on movie and television soundtracks and music for commercials, in addition to music for bands. Some session musicians are members of orchestras that play classical music. A seat on an orchestra pays very

A session musician plays his guitar during a recording session.

well, and competition can be fierce. Session musicians need to be easygoing and able to adapt to new situations quickly, because they are often given music that they have never seen before and are asked to play it in a short time.

Some professional musicians are known as general musicians. These musicians have learned a variety of songs, usually popular songs written by other people, from many periods of popular music. This is called their repertoire. A repertoire is like a music résumé; general musicians use

Musicians who can read and write music are likely to get more session work than those who can't.

their repertoire to obtain work at a variety of situations. General musicians can work alone or with a regular group of musicians and can play events such as weddings, birthday parties, and corporate functions.

A professional musician can also rely on his or her voice as an instrument. Professional singers' voices have many classifications that are organized by vocal range, (soprano, contralto, tenor, and baritone) or by style of music. People who sing professionally also need to be

able to read music; the human voice is an instrument that requires as much training to "play" as does, say, a cello.

Education and Training

You don't need to attend music school to be a musician, but some training is definitely required to work professionally. If you have some experience, the first step you may want to take is to join the band at your school or in your community, or to take private lessons outside of school. If you want to sing, join the choir or audition for a school play or musical. If your school doesn't offer these activities, you may want to look outside the academic world and in the direction of semiprofessional performance, such as summer stock plays or smaller, independent productions.

If you don't go to college, it may be a good idea to take a few classes in some important areas of music. Most music played today has roots in classical music—that could be a good place to start. Remember, the later you start, the more difficult the path to success may be.

You need to be able to read music and be highly skilled at playing an instrument in order to be a member of a professional orchestra.

Salary

The average annual salary for musicians and singers is about $30,000, but this figure can vary. There are plenty of things that factor into what you can make as a musician, including your résumé (where you've worked before), reputation, and the hours you are available to work. Some musicians work as session musicians and general musicians at the same time. Doing multiple jobs can definitely increase what you will make. Many musicians teach privately to supplement their incomes. Members of orchestras make anywhere from $21,000 and up per year and belong to local chapters of a union. The smaller the orchestra and the region, the fewer number of performances, meaning a lower salary.

The average musician doesn't strike it rich. People who play music professionally do it because they love what they do. There is often downtime in between jobs for musicians, and many encounter unemployment while waiting for the next job.

Outlook

As we said earlier, the environment for performing musicians is highly competitive. Many aspects of the music business are very attractive; performing as a musician to crowds and playing with other talented musicians falls into the same category. If this is the route you choose, make yourself as marketable as possible. Learn additional instruments and, most of all, practice. According to the *2001 Occupational Outlook Handbook*, musician jobs are expected to grow at an average rate for the next few years. What does that mean to you? People like live music; as long as they do, professional musicians will be needed.

Additional Information

Most musicians work odd hours, which means late nights and weekends—these are the times when most people choose to seek out entertainment. This is another job that requires you to be a "people person." Musicians have to know how to get along with other people, both in bands they may play with, and with an audience. Shy people may want to reconsider a career as a professional musician. Geography makes a difference, too. It's easier to find work as a session musician, for instance, if you live in or near a city that has more recording facilities than a small town may. New York, Nashville, and Los Angeles may provide you with more opportunities to audition and find work than smaller towns will.

FOR MORE INFORMATION

ASSOCIATIONS

Creative Musicians Coalition

1024 W. Willcox Avenue
Peoria, IL 61604
(309) 685-4843
e-mail: info@aimcmc.com
Web site: http://www.aimcmc.com
The CMC is an international organization dedicated to the advancement of new music and the success of the independent musician.

Music and Entertainers Independent Student Association (MEISA)

Web site: http://www.wiu.edu/users/mimusba/meisa
This is a global organization of students working with educators and professionals from the music industry to prepare for careers in music.

WEB SITES

Canadian Musician

http://www.canadianmusician.com
Canadian Musician is a print magazine, but its Web site also has some material from past issues, including networking information for musicians to meet one another.

Carol Kaye's Web Site

http://www.carolkaye.com.
Carol Kaye is the First Lady of the bass guitar, an instrument not many women are famous for playing. She has great advice for musicians and her story is interesting to read. She actually became a session player by accident!

Internet Music Resource Guide
http://www.specialweb.com/music
Links to Internet sites that are music resources.

Musician.com
http://www.musician.com.
A great Web site dedicated to all forms of musicianship, including performing, recording, and songwriting.

Sonic State
http://www.sonicstate.com
Links to music resources on the Internet.

BOOKS

DeSantis, Jayce. *How to Run a Recording Session*. Emeryville, CA: Mix Books, 1997.
It's best to know what to expect when you enter the recording studio. This book includes information on studio engineering.

Halloran, Mark. *The Musician's Business and Legal Guide*. Upper Saddle River, NJ: Prentice Hall, 2001.
Twenty-two entertainment lawyers break down legalese into language everyone can understand.

Kashif and Gary Greenberg. *Everything You'd Better Know About the Record Industry*. Venice, CA: Brooklyn Boy Books, 1996.
This is a comprehensive guide for anyone who wants to pursue a career in the music industry. Rapper Ice Cube calls it the new recording industry bible.

Krasilovsky, M. William, Sidney Shemel, and John Gross. *This Business of Music: The Definitive Guide to the Music Industry*. New York: Watson-Guptill Publishers, 2000.
This is a comprehensive reference to the economic, legal, and financial aspects of the music business. It's known as the definitive book on the music industry.

Lathrop, Tad, and Jim Pettigrew. *This Business of Music Marketing and Promotion*. New York: Billboard Books, 1999.
This is a guide to planning and producing a complete marketing campaign for selling music to the listening public.

Passman, Donald S. *All You Need to Know About the Music Business*. New York: Simon and Schuster, 2000.
This book gives advice about negotiating deals, advisers, publishing, touring, and merchandising. It includes helpful information for anyone interested in pursuing a career in the music industry.

Rapaport, Diane Sward. *How to Make and Sell Your Own Recording*. Upper Saddle River, NJ: Prentice Hall, 1999.
This book gives guidance on recording, pricing product, and selling your recordings via the Internet.

Schulenberg, Richard. *Legal Aspects of the Record Industry: An Insider's View*. New York: Billboard Books, 1999.
Here's an overview of all things legal with regards to the music industry. It includes annotated examples of contracts.

Schwartz, Daylle Deanna. *The Real Deal: How to Get Signed to a Record Label from A–Z*. New York: Billboard Books, 1997.
This book gives insider information on launching a recording career.

Spellman, Peter. *The Self-Promoting Musician: Strategies for Independent Music Success*. Boston: Berklee Press Publications, 2000.
This book gives valuable guidance about adding all-important business expertise to artistic talent when pursuing a career as a musician.

Stim, Richard. *Music Law: How to Run Your Band's Business*. Berkeley, CA: Nolo Press, 2001.
Here's helpful advice from a musician and an attorney about the legal side of music.

Sweeney, Tim, and Mark Geller. *Tim Sweeney's Guide to Releasing Independent Records*. Torrance, CA: T.S.A. Books, 1996.
This book teaches the reader how to set up his or her own independent label, produce records, get distribution into major retail outlets, design a promotional strategy, and get records played.

MUSIC BROADCASTER

Music broadcasters, simply put, work together to create the programs you hear on the radio. The effort of many people collaborating, or working together, is absolutely necessary to make sure that music gets from the artist to the general public. Thanks to technology, there are many opportunities to work in music broadcasting, such as radio and Internet stations.

Announcers are the people whose voices represent a station. They sometimes are known as radio personalities or DJs (a little different than the DJs we've already talked about). Announcers can introduce news, weather, and, most important to us, music. Unfortunately, most DJs on the air don't get to pick what they want to play. Instead, they are usually given a playlist by programming directors, who decide what a station is going to play, based on the station's format, or music type. How many formats are there? Turn on your radio and turn the dial—every type of music is represented, from country to rock to rap to dance. Some smaller radio stations and Internet music sites are free-form, which means they may not play only one sort of music. These are great places to work if you want to learn about a large range of music types.

Music directors are in charge of keeping a station's music catalog, or library, up-to-date as new recordings are released by record companies. The playlist of a station is always changing, which can be both exciting and frustrating at the same time. Every week, the programming director and music director (sometimes it's the same person) decide which songs to drop or add from the station's playlist.

Despite their popularity with the listening public, most radio DJs have little influence on the radio station's playlist.

Guess what? Radio stations also need sound engineers! People who listen to the radio want what they hear to sound good, just like concert-goers or people who want to see a Broadway show or buy a new record. Luckily, many parts of the music business are so related that with experience and training, people can do many jobs at once or move from one area to another. It takes more than one engineer to make a station run. Often, a few sound engineers will work for the chief engineer of a station, who is responsible for all of the technical aspects of a broadcast, to make sure sounds travel from the microphone to the radio speaker to our ears.

The jobs that are available in music broadcasting touch on many aspects of a business. Radio stations need people to write material for the DJs, to maintain the station's electronic equipment, and to sell advertising time to businesses who want to promote their companies.

Education and Training

Although colleges offer broadcasting degrees, you can still gain entry into the world of broadcasting without one; however, it will be more difficult to do so. People with computer skills are at an advantage here; more and more radio outfits are becoming increasingly digital and computerized. Take advantage of computer programs your school may have. After school, you may want to invest in some basic broadcasting courses at a local college to get a better understanding of the technical side of the industry. There are also broadcasting schools that offer one- or two-year programs in all aspects of the business.

Without a bachelor's degree in broadcasting, it is a little more difficult to break into the announcing side of radio. Experience is as important as a college degree in some aspects of the radio business, so try to obtain as much as possible while you're still in school. If you want to be an on-air personality, get involved in activities at your school that are related, such as the debate team, school plays, or announcing for the football or the basketball teams.

Some radio stations at colleges and small local stations need volunteers or interns to help out in the off months. This is free training! Use this opportunity to get involved early; it will pay off, even if you don't get a paycheck for the time you spend learning part of the trade. The more motivation you display as an intern may make the difference between being hired or not for a paying job down the road.

Salary

If you're interning to gain on-the-job training, there is no pay; this is definitely a profession that requires experience before you can rely on it as a steady source of income. For paid employees, salaries vary, depending on the particular job a person does.

Radio deejays must often stick to a playlist set by their program directors.

The average hourly rate for announcers is approximately fifteen dollars. Popular music personalities make more than this, but to reach that level takes a little time. Salaries for behind-the-scenes people like technicians vary according to time in the position and experience.

Outlook

Employment opportunities in standard radio announcing are expected to decline slightly in the next few years. Not many new stations are starting up, and many are down-sizing or merging with other stations. Two areas to explore may be Internet radio, which broadcasts to computers, and satellite radio, which beams radio programs directly to people's automobiles.

FOR MORE INFORMATION

ASSOCIATIONS AND PLACES OF INTEREST
Museum of Television and Radio

In New York:
25 West 52nd Street
New York, NY 10019
(212) 621-6600
Web site: http://www.mtr.org

In Los Angeles:
465 North Beverly Drive
Beverly Hills, CA 90210
(310) 786-1025
Web site: http://www.mtr.org
This museum—one branch in Los Angeles, the other in New York City—collects and preserves radio programs and makes them available to the public. The museum also puts together interesting exhibitions.

National Association of Broadcasters (NAB)
1771 N Street NW
Washington, DC 20036
(202) 429-5300
e-mail: nab@nab.org
Web site: http://www.nab.org
This is a full-service trade association that promotes and protects the interests of radio and television broadcasters around the world.

WEB SITES

BE Radio
http://www.beradio.com
This is a full-service online industry magazine with excellent editorials, features, news, issues, product reviews, and other important information regarding the radio industry.

Inside Radio
http://www.insideradio.com
This online magazine is updated frequently and has the latest on what's happening on the business side of the radio industry. It also looks at important people in the business. Overall, this is a good starting point to learn some terms and facts about commercial radio.

Radio Locator
http://www.radio-locator.com
This is a search engine that allows you to search for any radio station broadcasting in the United States by music type. You can also search for any station broadcasting music over the Internet worldwide. Did you ever wonder what's big in Bolivia or France? Check out this site.

Radio Online
http://www.radioonline.com
Radio Online covers news, trends, ratings, and everything else you can think of in the radio industry. It also posts job openings around the country.

Ruffsounds.com
http://www.ruffsounds.com
Designed specifically for radio talent, this site helps radio broadcasters find the information they need for their shows, such as news, entertainment and music happenings, humor, and soundbites.

BOOKS

Staff, Mike. *How to Become a Radio DJ: A Guide to Breaking and Entering*. Troy, MI: Happy Communications, 1998.
This book suggests strategies for breaking into the world of radio deejaying. Check out www.djbook.com for information.

EDUCATION/TRAINING

Noncollege broadcast schools are available throughout the United States and Canada. Following are a few correspondence programs that offer distance-learning courses and local internships and apprenticeships.

Air Time Radio Broadcasting School
(800) 345-2344
Web site: http://www.broadcasting-school.com
This school offers a comprehensive list of courses relating to radio broadcasting and placement in internships all over the country.

Broadcast School in a Box
Web site: http://www.broadcastschool.com
This is a program that you can do at home, even while holding another job. Students are hooked up with internships in their area, because experience is the best way to get a job in radio broadcasting. Check out the Web site for testimonials from people who have benefited from this program.

Get a Mentor—Apprentice Mentor Association
Web site: http://www.getamentor.com
This organization sets up its students with apprenticeships in the radio business. The idea is that working closely with a mentor will

teach the student more than he or she would learn in a classroom, and also that he or she would be a more attractive candidate for future jobs, having had the benefit of a mentor.

FOR FUN

Airheads **(1994)**
Twentieth Century Fox
Brendan Fraser and Steve Buscemi play two band members who really (really) understand the wide audience you can reach via the radio waves.

FM **(1978)**
Universal Studios Home Video
Kind of dated, but a good look at the bad side of the radio industry.

Pump Up the Volume **(1990)**
New Line Cinema
Christian Slater stars in this movie about a high school kid who starts a pirate radio station in his basement.

INSTRUMENT TECHNICIAN

Instrument technicians are people who specialize in one or more types of services that they provide to touring companies. They're often nicknamed "roadies," and they are the backbone of musical and theatrical companies that hit the road and travel all over the world to bring entertainment to the public.

A pair of roadies transports musical equipment to a concert site.

Description

Roadies have training and expertise in certain areas connected with live performances, such as lighting, sound (see audio engineer), stage design, and instruments, to name a few. Instrument technicians also support touring musical groups in ways we rarely think of. They take care of costumes and food. They drive the band bus and the truck containing the equipment. Depending on the size of the operation, a crew of instrument technicians can range from two men who are responsible for all of the technical support to hundreds of members of a support staff.

If you decide to become a roadie, you are really becoming a kind of performer. Singers can't be heard if the speakers don't work, and they can't be seen if the spotlights are burnt out. Instrument technicians perform, but they do their best work where no one in the audience can see them. If you can play an instrument well, but are not interested in being the person in front of the crowd, you may want to try your hand at being an instrument technician. Can't play an instrument? That's not a problem. There are plenty of other jobs that help shows or performances run, so you could see which ones interest you most.

Instrument technicians can obtain work on a local or regional level, as well as on a national level. Local work is close to home and involves helping out local bands or providing technical support for the community theater group. Check local papers and music magazines to see who may need help in your area. The regional level is more involved. First, it involves traveling, which is one way to see another part of the country while you work. Regional tech crews are small (two to three people) and assist bands or touring companies of Broadway shows, for example. Working at the regional level usually requires experience, which can be gained locally. Occasionally, however, regional companies will take on

A young instrument technician monitors the sound and lights before a nightclub performance.

apprentices to train. The national level (sometimes international, too) is where the best technicians find work. At this stage, level of technical skill is very high; the chances of being away for long periods of time is even higher. Some jobs can even involve prolonged travel in another country.

One of the keys to being an instrument technician is dedication. It may take some time to progress from working locally to working nationally, but persistence pays off. The more you work at a local or a regional level, the more people you will meet who may be able to help you find work with a traveling company.

Education and Training

Unfortunately, there is no such thing as roadie school. To become an instrument technician, start in high school by working as a stagehand for a school or a local production to decide whether or not you would like to pursue that sort of work once you graduate. This a great time to learn the basics and to find out where your talent lies. You also can contact the local branch of the International Alliance of Theatrical Stage Employees (IATSE), or a professional sound and lighting company and intern for them. The more training and/or experience a person gains before finishing high school, the better.

Salary

The pay varies for each level of work, as well as for particular jobs; some bands or companies may pay more than others. At the regional level, techs usually get paid per gig, so unless you work every night, the work is definitely part-time. As roadies move to higher levels of responsibility the pay will increase, and so will the hours.

Additional Information

Traveling and working with a bunch of people for a prolonged period of time means that an instrument technician has to be able to work well with other people. Everyone who works for a band or on the crew of a touring show should have the same goal: the best performance possible every time. And remember that tours can go on for months. Sometimes your ability to get along with people may be just as valuable as the technical skill you've been hired for. Being stuck on a bus with the same people for months is a skill in itself! The work is hard but rewarding if you ultimately want the chance to travel and live an unusual lifestyle. If you don't feel that you could be a team player, then this may not be the job for you.

FOR MORE INFORMATION

ASSOCIATIONS
The International Alliance of Theatrical Stage Employees (IATSE)
Moving Picture Technicians, Artists and Allied Crafts
1515 Broadway
Suite 601
New York, NY 10036
(212) 730-1770
Web site: http://www.iatse.lm.com.
According to its site, the IATSE is "the labor union representing technicians, artisans and craftspersons in the entertainment industry, including live theatre, film and television production, and trade shows."

WEB SITES

Applause Music Careers
http://www.cnvi.com/applause
This Web site is a great resource of any aspect of the industry, but has an especially good section on instrument technicians.

Backstage World
http://www.backstageworld.com.
Backstage World is another Web site dedicated to support staff.

Pro Lights and Staging
http://www.plsn.com
News, reviews, interviews, features, and more than you ever knew about what goes on behind the scenes all can be found here.

Roadie.net
http://www.roadie.net
A companion to Karl Kuenning's book, *Roadie: A True Story*, this Web site tells you everything you want to know about the life of a roadie, including job details, news, gig postings, advice on breaking into the business, roadie lingo, and message boards.

Roadogz
http://www.roadogz.com
Billed as "survival for the people on the road in the entertainment industry," this Web site posts articles, editorials, stories, product reviews, message boards, and even games and travel information— anything of interest to people working on the technical side of the entertainment business.

Rock the Roadie
http://www.rocktheroadie.com
Created by a veteran roadie, this Web site serves as an advertisement for *The Roadie Guidebook,* the practical manual for anyone who dreams of following their favorite band around the world.

Stagespecs.com
http://www.stagespecs.com
All kinds of resources for theatrical and stage professionals. This site has job postings, industry news, and important links.

Tour Support.net
http://www.toursupport.net
This Web site is the self-described "Online Home of Touring Professionals." It offers weather forecasts, games, and tips for those who earn their living on the road. Check out the message board for job openings.

BOOKS

Carter, Paul. *The Backstage Handbook: An Illustrated Almanac of Technical Information*. New York: Broadway Press, 1994.

Kuenning, Karl. *Roadie: A True Story (At Least The Parts I Remember)*. New York: Writer's Showcase, 2001.
A true account of the trials and tribulations of a traveling roadie/instrument technician from the 1970s to the 1980s.

Reid, Francis. *The ABC of Stage Technology*. London: A & C Black, 1995. Basic information about working on the stage.

BOOKING AGENT/CLUB MANAGER

Live music is a popular and important form of entertainment for both spectators and performers. Music fans go to clubs and stadiums to see bands perform live. Talent scouts in the entertainment business often travel to live events to see artists they may want to sign. Musicians themselves tour to make an important portion of their

A club manager discusses the lineup of upcoming events with the club's booking agent, DJ, and security personnel.

income. Who makes sure that all of these people have a place to go? Club managers and booking agents do.

Description

Club managers do what their title suggests—they take care of the day-to-day details of keeping a venue open and letting people hear live music. The list of responsibilities is large: Hiring and paying employees, paying bills, and keeping order are just a few. A manager's job is to manage all of the resources he or she has to help things run as smoothly as possible on any given night of the week. Some places that host live music also serve food and alcohol, which can make things more complicated in terms of licensing. Most businesses are licensed by a city or a state; there are dozens of types of licenses, from food to alcohol. Many cities even require a license for clubs to allow dancing! If you manage a club, you'll have to maintain a budget. Businesses can only spend as much money as they make, and everything costs money, from payrolls to licenses to heating bills.

Booking agents at live venues are in charge of booking, or scheduling, live music. Booking shows can be difficult. In larger cities, there can be competition among clubs to book certain artists who are very likely to draw large crowds, which really means more money. Booking agents also have to possess budgeting skills. Musicians charge money for performances, and they can't play a venue if the money earned isn't enough to cover their own costs (such as gas, car repairs, and backup singers). If a booking agent books a show and is unable to pay a band because of the club's costs (like ticket takers and sound engineers), his or her reputation could be damaged. Over time, this results in decreased ability to attract bands with higher profiles.

In some clubs, the manager and the booking agent are the same person. This equals a big responsibility, but it also

Booking agents schedule talent at theaters, universities, music venues, and comedy clubs.

keeps everything under the control of one person, which can eliminate possible conflicts. For example, if one person books shows for a venue and another person manages that venue, misunderstandings could be more likely to happen.

In addition to clubs that specifically feature music, booking agents and club managers can also find employment opportunities at local theaters, comedy or variety clubs, and private and public colleges and universities. Musicians may not play consistently at these places, but the experience can lead to a job dealing specifically with music.

Education and Training

There is no school that can teach booking or club managing. Yes, some community colleges and local institutions offer small business courses, but they aren't specifically suited to this job. What you will need is experience. Many people in this field start at entry level, performing smaller tasks to help with the overall running of a club or a venue.

Any job related to the venue can provide you with valuable experience; it takes more than one person to help a show or a concert run smoothly. The club manager or booking agent needs people to take tickets, watch the door, and promote shows, to name just a few duties. It definitely takes time to be able to call a popular band's manager and set up a performance.

Like most really interesting and challenging jobs involving music, you have to work your way up by taking jobs that in themselves aren't that exciting. They will, however, give you experience, allow you to watch how things work, and let you see how certain decisions affect the outcome of a particular problem or situation.

Salary

The salaries of booking agents and club managers vary, depending on a few things. One is venue size: Bigger places hold more people and sell more tickets. Another is reputation: Clubs with credibility can draw more popular acts. Many managers and booking agents get a set salary and are sometimes rewarded with a small percentage, or commission, of the total profit resulting from a particular performance.

Outlook

As long as people still want to hear live music, there will be a need for people to coordinate performances. The *2001 Occupational Outlook Handbook* expects average growth for musicians, which translates to about the same or a little less for the people who schedule their performances.

Profile

Ten Questions with Todd Abramson

Owner/Booking Agent, Maxwell's, Hoboken, New Jersey

HOW DID YOU GET INVOLVED WITH LIVE MUSIC?

Well, I started coordinating live shows when I was in high school. I'd have local bands play in my basement when my parents went away for the weekend. When I moved east, I had a friend in New York who was a musician and suggested I try my hand booking shows part-time at a club called Folk City.

HOW LONG HAVE YOU BEEN AT YOUR CURRENT JOB?

On and off for fifteen years. The original owner sold the bar, and I had the chance to buy it with some other investors a few years ago. I've been booking shows since I've worked here, though.

WHAT DO YOU THINK IS THE KEY TO SUCCESS IN YOUR LINE OF WORK?

Mainly, exude calm at all times. If you have a crisis, freaking out about it will only make matters worse. Remember that somebody has to keep a clear head.

IS IT HARD TO BE BOTH BOOKER AND MANAGER?

Sometimes it is, but in tough situations, the booker and manager have to support one another and not argue or have conflicts, so I guess in that respect, it's easier to do both jobs.

DO YOU HAVE MUCH FINANCIAL RESPONSIBILITY?

Yes!!! My partner helps out, but I usually handle the day-to-day stuff like budgets and salaries.

WHAT IS YOUR ADVICE TO SOMEONE WHO WOULD LIKE TO DO WHAT YOU DO?

Start early. Get involved, stick around, and show people you're dependable. Employers reward good employees, and they really reward good employees they can trust. Be a self-starter.

WHAT'S THE BEST WAY TO GET BOOKING CONNECTIONS?

First, go to shows. If you see a band you like, talk to them and start to develop a relationship. If they live far away, e-mail them. It's easier to network now than it was when I started. Most bands have a Web site, too. Use that to your advantage—be aggressive!

WHAT IF YOU'RE UNDER TWENTY-ONE?

That can be an obstacle, but there are still places that put on shows for people under the drinking age. We do shows like that here sometimes. The connections may be fewer, but the same rules apply.

IS YOUR JOB CHALLENGING?

Sometimes. Angry road managers, staffing problems, and unruly crowds are tough enough alone, but when they all happen together, that's when it's challenging.

DO YOU LIKE YOUR JOB?

I wouldn't be doing it otherwise.

FOR MORE INFORMATION

WEB SITES

Internet Music Resource Guide
http://www.specialweb.com/music
This is a reference of links and other resources to Internet sites about music.

Taxi
http://www.taxi.com
(800) 458-2111
This is the site for an independent artists and repertoire company helping unsigned bands, artists, and songwriters get deals and promotions. Also helpful for industry listings.

BOOKS

Frascogna, Xavier M., and H. Lee Hetherington. *This Business of Artist Management*. New York: Billboard Books, 1997.
This Business of Artist Management will help anyone intending to work with musicians for a living.

Kashif and Gary Greenberg. *Everything You'd Better Know About the Record Industry*. Venice, CA: Brooklyn Boy Books, 1996.
This is a comprehensive guide for anyone who wants to pursue a career in the music industry. Rapper Ice Cube calls it the new bible for the recording industry.

Krasilovsky, M. William, Sidney Shemel, and John Gross. *This Business of Music: The Definitive Guide to the Music Industry*. New York: Watson-Guptill Publishers, 2000.
This is a comprehensive reference to the economic, legal, and financial aspects of the music business. It's known as the definitive book on the music industry.

Passman, Donald S. *All You Need to Know About the Music Business*. New York: Simon and Schuster, 2000.
This book gives advice about negotiating deals, advisers, publishing, touring, and merchandising. It includes helpful information for anyone interested in pursuing a career in the music industry.

PERIODICALS

Alternative Press
Web site: http://www.altpress.com
Alternative Press features reviews, news, and features for fans of alternative, indie, ska, electronic, dub, industrial, punk, techno, underground, rock, ambient, and experimental music.

Pollstar
4697 W. Jacquelyn Avenue
Fresno, CA 93722
(559) 271-7900
Web site: http://www.pollstar.com
A print magazine with an online component, *Pollstar* publishes concert tour schedules for music professionals.

MUSIC PROMOTER

One way to stay connected to music is to help spread the word about it. If you like to talk about who's who in music and what they're doing, you can turn this desire into another employment option. The average person doesn't have the opportunity to keep up to date on every single record or CD coming out every week on the hundreds of record labels

that exist in the United States and Europe and other parts of the world. This is where music promotion steps in.

Description

Promotion companies are independent companies that work with record labels, management, and artists to increase public knowledge of a particular song, record, album, or musician. The key word in this line of work is publicity. People who work in promotions are mostly concerned with making their client or project as public and well-known as possible.

There are many levels of promotion in which you can involve yourself. Some promotions are very grassroots, meaning they are very local yet very effective. An example of this would be an independent street team, similar to street teams used by many record distribution companies. This can be known as guerrilla promotions; starting with the average person to get the word out in a natural way has proved to work very well. If you take a walk around any midsized city, you'll be sure to see posters or stickers advertising a band or a musician. Those advertisements are the direct result of guerrilla promotions.

Street teams are responsible for the promotional posters often seen on scaffolding boards and in store windows.

The Internet is ideal for promotions. For every person who lives in a city or an urban area, there is someone in a smaller town who may not have immediate access to entertainment; however, many people either own a computer or have access to one with Internet capabilities. Promotion companies use the Internet and e-mail to inform people of upcoming tours, recordings, and general news involving their clients.

On a larger scale, bigger promotion companies may work directly with a record label to develop a general marketing strategy to get word to the public about a musical act. Bigger labels have more money to use to promote their artists, which makes it easier to get the word out than, for instance, a local artist who may not have the resources to take out television and radio ads to promote himself or herself.

Music promotion companies use unique or memorable items to make both their client and their client's music more memorable. These can range from stickers with a band logo on them to an added value gift to encourage people to buy an artist's record. Some promotion companies are very innovative and take the guerrilla marketing approach for more well-known clients by doing things locally, like painting a car with the name and picture of an artist, or something even more unusual.

Many promotion companies use a combination of all of the above—the Internet, e-mail, patches, stickers, as well as the old-fashioned approach of calling record stores, radio

Janet Jackson greets fans outside a New York music store as she arrives for an in-store promotion of her album, *Velvet Rope*.

stations, and DJs to inform them of new developments. Even though this is the computer age, many people still like personal interactions with one another; many businesses try to combine the old and the new to take promotions into the twenty-first century.

Education and Training

As with most jobs in the music business, there aren't any academic programs that specifically teach music promotions.

Rawkus Records

Rawkus Records, a New York City–based rap and hip-hop label, completely understands the importance of using as many resources as possible to spread the word on the street about their label and their clients. During warmer months, Rawkus employees cruise the avenues and streets of New York in a hand-painted ice-cream truck! Better yet, they actually serve ice cream. The truck carries the names of rappers on the label, especially those with new albums that are about to be released. The driver also carries special promotional materials for anyone who'd like to find out more about Rawkus clients.

There is huge potential for this promotion to gain more recognition for Rawkus artists—someone may never have heard a single record the label puts out, but one thing is certain: Everybody likes ice cream. Combining certain types of music with other consumable promotions is not new, but the people at Rawkus managed a new twist on the formula.

However, many community colleges offer basic marketing courses, which provide solid backgrounds in the principles behind promotion. A sure way to become a part of this side of the music business is to intern part-time to gain some knowledge about the general goings-on until a paid position opens up. Many people who work in publicity have formerly worked at record labels or record stores, and have learned a little about promotions that way. Some people even decide to branch out and start their own promotion companies after they have learned the basics from a larger company.

Salary

Salary depends on the promotions company and its size. A company with many clients will pay more, but will probably require you to work longer hours, and the pressure could be much greater than at a smaller firm. Part of your salary may also depend on your personal ability to attract and produce results for certain clients. The best way to find out a particular salary would be to contact individual companies at both ends of the size spectrum.

Outlook

As long as musicians and bands want to attract listeners, they will most likely need assistance in making that a reality.

The music business is constantly changing, so the outlook is fair to good. Again, it is usually easy to obtain an internship, but it is more difficult to be taken on by any company as a part-time or a full-time employee.

FOR MORE INFORMATION

WEB SITES

Girlie Action
http://www.girlieaction.com
This is the site for a New York City–based public relations and marketing business.

Holiday Matinee
http://www.holidaymatinee.com
This is the site for some music promoters based in San Diego.

Internet Music Resource Guide
http://www.specialweb.com/music
This is a reference of links and other resources to Internet sites about music.

Melting Vinyl
http://www.meltingvinyl.co.uk
Melting Vinyl is an English company that promotes all kinds of music. Check out their site to learn about the work involved.

Open Directory Project
http://dmoz.org/arts/music/resources
This is a volunteer Web directory with information about loads of things. Their Musician's Resource links are very helpful.

BOOKS

Frascogna, Xavier M., and H. Lee Hetherington. *This Business of Artist Management.* New York: Billboard Books, 1997.
This Business of Artist Management will help anyone intending to work with musicians for a living.

Kashif and Gary Greenberg. *Everything You'd Better Know About the Record Industry*. Venice, CA: Brooklyn Boy Books, 1996.
This is a comprehensive guide for anyone who wants to pursue a career in the music industry. Rapper Ice Cube calls it the new bible for the recording industry.

Krasilovsky, M. William, Sidney Shemel, and John Gross. *This Business of Music: The Definitive Guide to the Music Industry*. New York: Watson-Guptill Publishers, 2000.
This is a comprehensive reference to the economic, legal, and financial aspects of the music business. It's known as the definitive book on the music industry.

Lathrop, Tad, and Jim Pettigrew. *This Business of Music Marketing and Promotion*. New York: Billboard Books, 1999.
A guide to planning and producing a complete marketing campaign for selling music to the listening public.

Passman, Donald S. *All You Need to Know About the Music Business*. New York: Simon and Schuster, 2000.
This book offers advice about negotiating deals, advisers, publishing, touring, and merchandising. It is helpful information for anyone interested in pursuing a career in the music industry.

Pettigrew, Jim. *The Billboard Guide to Music Publicity*. New York: Watson-Guptill Publishers, 1997.
The Billboard Guide to Music Publicity informs the reader about how to create press kits and other ways to get the word out about a musician or a band.

PERIODICALS

Alternative Press
Web site: http://www.altpress.com
Alternative Press features reviews, news, and features for fans of alternative, indie, ska, electronic, dub, industrial, punk, techno, underground, rock, ambient, and experimental music.

Billboard
1515 Broadway
New York, NY 10036
(212) 764-7300
Web site: http://www.billboard.com
Billboard is a very well-known weekly magazine dealing with the music industry. It covers all bases, such as independent music and world music.

Pollstar
4697 W. Jacquelyn Avenue
Fresno, CA 93722
(559) 271-7900
Web site: http://www.pollstar.com
A print magazine with an online component, *Pollstar* publishes concert tour schedules for music professionals.

10

INSTRUMENT REPAIRER AND TUNER

Musicians play the instruments, but who keeps them running and sounding good? What if a piano is out of tune? What does a violinist do if his or her violin is broken? What does a trumpeter do with a dented horn? They all call on instrument repairers and tuners.

Description

Music repair and tuning requires a greater deal of skill and training than many of the jobs described in this book. People who perform this work usually develop a large body of knowledge about a particular type of instrument, rather than attempt to repair every instrument under the sun. People who want their pianos tuned don't call tuba repairers—they call an expert on pianos.

There are four major types of instruments that people repair: piano/organ, band, violin, and guitar. Although guitars and violins both have strings, they are very different in many other ways. Therefore, special attention is needed for each musical instrument.

Piano and organ repairers and tuners have to deal with the thousands (that's correct, thousands) of parts that make up the average piano if keys stick or do not move when pressed. If you were to look inside a piano, you would notice dozens of strings. To tune a piano, each string has to be adjusted individually. This usually takes about two hours on the average.

Piano repair and tuning is a painstaking process. The repairer needs to know not only the relationships between keys and strings, but also the proper sound of each key.

Band instruments are those instruments played by traditional orchestras, rather than those used by a rock band with guitars and amplifiers. Band instruments include brass and wind instruments, as well as percussion instruments. Brass and wind instruments are blown through, and include tubas, trumpets, trombones, oboes, cornets, French horns, flugelhorns, saxophones, contrabasoons . . . The list could go on for a long time.

In order to know what's wrong with an instrument, a repairer needs to know how to play that instrument. Repairers and tuners also perform the important task of cleaning musical equipment. Brass and wind instruments have many moving parts that could stick or prevent air from passing through them correctly if dirt and dust were to accumulate over a long time.

Percussion instruments are instruments that have skin stretched over a frame and are tapped to make sounds: snare drums, congas, tympani, and bongos all fall into this category. Repair persons may have to cut and stretch a new skin over a snare drum, adjust its tension, or repair cracks in cymbals.

A repairman examines an out-of-tune cello. Like all instrument tuners, he can play the instruments he works on.

Violin tuners tune and repair violins and other stringed instruments that are played with a bow, such as cellos and violas (larger violins with a deeper sound). Guitar tuners and repairers do the same thing to electric and acoustic guitars, as well as to bass guitars and other variations on non-bowed stringed instruments.

In addition to the main categories, there are other instruments that require special and singular attention, such as pipe organs, electronic organs, and electronic keyboards.

Musical instrument repairers and tuners often work alone and in a relatively quiet environment in order to tune instruments as well as they possibly can. This type of work is not recommended for those who like to be on the go and meet people during the course of a workday. Tuners and repairers can work in a variety of locales, including repair shops and music stores. Piano tuners often have to travel to do their work, since the instruments are difficult to move.

Education and Training

This is one line of work that requires extensive training, and it must be hands-on. Most places that hire tuners and repairers prefer their employees to have schooling of some sort. Many community colleges and music schools offer coursework in instrument repair and tuning for the categories mentioned above. Instrument repair schools offer specific training and require one or two years of study.

Without schooling, it is still possible to succeed as a repairer or a tuner. The way to do this is through an apprenticeship, which is a more professional version of an internship. The key is to start now if this is a career you're considering. The number of repairers and tuners who take on assistants or apprentices is very low, and the later you start, the tougher it's going to be. There are still a few places that do offer on-the-job instruction to trainees. Usually, trainees perform another task while they learn a trade. For example, a trainee at a musical instrument store might sell sheet music or stock inventory while he or she is learning the ropes of repair with an expert. On the average, training in this way can take anywhere from two to five years. Interested? Start soon!

Salary

Instrument tuners and repairers can make as much as $38,000 per year, provided they work in urban areas where there are more live performances, orchestras, and musicians who need to have their instruments worked on. The average salary is around $23,000 per year.

Outlook

Repair and tuning jobs, according to the *2001 Occupational Outlook Handbook*, are expected to increase at a rate that is lower than the average for the next few years. This is even more of a reason to get involved at an earlier age if you feel like this is an avenue of employment that you may want to pursue. Since training takes some time, job openings come and go at a slower rate than that of other professions. The more training a person has will make him or her all the more valuable in the next few years.

FOR MORE INFORMATION

ASSOCIATIONS

Musical Instrument Technicians Association (MITA)
(800) 942-7870
e-mail: info@mitatechs.com
Web site: http://www.mitatechs.com
MITA is an association of worldwide professional technicians organized to improve the electronic music service industry

National Association of Professional Band Instrument Repair Technicians (NAPBIRT)
P.O. Box 51
Normal, IL 61761
(309) 452-4257
e-mail: napbirt@napbirt.org
Web site: http://www.napbirt.org

This is the association for band instrument repairers. NAPBIRT is a valuable resource for news and information regarding instrument repair and also training and apprenticeship opportunities for learning the craft.

Piano Technicians Guild (PTG)

3930 Washington Street
Kansas City, MO 64111-2963
(816) 753-7747
e-mail: ptg@ptg.org
Web site: http://www.ptg.org

PTG is a nonprofit association of piano technicians. The organization publishes the monthly *Piano Technicians Journal* and holds events and seminars for piano tuners and repairers.

WEB SITES

David T. Van Zandt

http://www.vanzandtviolins.com

David Van Zandt is a Seattle violin maker. His Web site lends insight into the world of someone who completely loves his work.

Instrument Repair Stuff

http://www.instrumentrepairstuff.com

This site is dedicated to supplying the repairer with the tools necessary to do the best job possible.

BOOKS

Brosnac, Donald. *Guitar Electronics for Musicians*. New York: Amsco Publications, 1983.
Guitar Electronics for Musicians will tell you everything you want to know about maintaining your electric guitar.

Burton, Stanley. *Instrument Repair for the Music Teacher*. New York: Alfred Publishing Company, 1978.
This book is a practical and comprehensive text on instrument repairs that commonly challenge the music teacher.

Cumpiano, William R., and Johnathan D. Natelson. *Guitarmaking Tradition and Technology: A Complete Reference for the Design and Construction of the Steel-String Folk Guitar and the Classical Guitar.* Amherst, MA: Rosewood Press, 1987.
This book includes all of the details you need to know to build your own classical or steel-stringed guitar. Information on suppliers, dimensions, and materials is indispensable.

Erlewine, Dan. *Guitar Player Repair Guide.* San Francisco, CA: GPI Books, 1990.
Guitar Player Repair Guide is a step-by-step manual to maintaining and repairing electric and acoustic guitars and basses. The book covers new tools and techniques, and provides detailed information on adjustments and repairs for specific models and manufacturers.

Fillet, Pieter J. *D.I.Y. Guitar Repair.* New York: Music Sales Corporation, 1984.
This is an invaluable manual for every guitarist. Diagrams and photos teach the reader how to carry out dozens of repairs including fixing loose frets, dealing with a warped neck, the correct way to put on new steel strings, adjusting the bridge, adjusting a guitar for lefthanded users, and more.

Hopkin, Bart. *Musical Instrument Design: Practical Information for Instrument Making.* Tuscon, AZ: See Sharp Press, 1996.
This book gives a comprehensive overview of design principles for acoustical instruments, with detailed illustrations.

Meyer, Raymond F. *Band Director's Guide to Instrument Repair.* New York: Alfred Publishing Company, 1973.
This is a practical guide with complete information on repairing band instruments right in the classroom.

Reblitz, Arthur A. *Piano Servicing, Tuning, and Rebuilding.* Vestal, NY: Vestal Press, 1993.
This is the ultimate reference book and instruction manual for both the professional and the amateur. This book examines different

styles of pianos and their parts and clearly instructs the reader in evaluating; cleaning and doing minor repairs; regulating; tuning theory and procedure; and complete restoration.

Wake, Harry Sebastian. *Violin Bow Rehair and Repair.* San Diego, CA: Harry S. Wake Publishing, 1997.
One of the best and easiest to understand manuals on the subject of rehairing, repairing, and restoring bows. The clearly written text is supplemented with eighty-eight photographs and drawings.

MUSIC
JOURNALIST

11

MUSIC JOURNALIST

As do many other writers and journalists, music journalists strive to
present a fair and accurate
representation of the facts,
whether they are related to
a record, a CD, or the scoop
behind a popular singer or
band. Music journalists get
the information and pass it
on. Jobs in music journalism

are not easy to get; they are relatively glamorous. Competition to be paid to meet popular musicians, see their shows, and talk to them about their records can be intense. If you have the drive to be on the go and the persistence to keep going in a competitive market, this may be a job to look into further.

Description

The majority of music journalists (also called music critics, rock critics, and music writers) basically perform a similar task—writing about music in some form. Some music writers review new records and CDs and inform the public as to whether they are good listening investments. New records are released every week, so there's usually something to write about. Record reviewers have to put personal preferences aside and give readers a fair and impartial viewpoint about what's on the market to hear.

Interviews are a big part of publicity for new albums. Many listeners want to know as much as possible about the bands and the musicians they follow. Via e-mail or armed with a tape recorder, interviewers talk to the people who make the records and try to put an interesting spin on a record many people may be writing about at the same time.

The movie *Almost Famous* is the story of a young music journalist who follows a band on tour. In the scene above, the legendary Lester Bangs (Philip Seymour Hoffman) gives advice to a novice writer (Patrick Fugit).

Education and Training

People who write about music have to be very knowledge-able about all types of music. They must also be good writers. College is not necessary, but it does help greatly; many music journalists have received degrees in journalism. Community colleges and local writing workshops do offer courses in writing, which can be very helpful in polishing your communication skills.

It's going to be hard to walk into the offices of *Vibe* or *Spin* and get a job as a writer—experience and longevity are what count. Start training on your own in high school. If your school has a newspaper, see if there are any openings that involve music writing. If your school doesn't offer a paper, try your hand at writing for a local arts paper or a newsletter. Take any writing jobs you have a chance to during this phase of your development. This will also give you a sizable portfolio. A portfolio is a résumé, or a listing of your qualifications as a writer—a collection of your work, to use as a sample to show prospective editors and employers. Magazines and e-zines (online magazines) don't hire without an idea of a person's writing skill and style. This is just like interning at a small record label with the hope of working for a major label at some point.

Working on your writing is another necessity here. In addition to classes in school, poke around on the Internet— almost every site related to music has a section that reviews records and CDs. Many don't pay. Even online music stores post reviews from customers, and that can be a good place to start. The idea is to have a collection of clips (published writing samples) to show to a potential employer. Take a look at the major music magazines at the local bookstore or magazine stand, and familiarize yourself with the kinds of records that get reviewed and the way in which they are reviewed. Finally, listen to as much music as you can. If you don't have a good working knowledge of music, you won't be able to succeed as a music critic.

Journalists interview rhythm and blues legends Fats Domino *(left)* and Ray Charles *(right)* at a restaurant.

Salary

The salary of music writers is largely freelance, meaning writers get paid an agreed-upon sum of money before they write a piece. The sum is usually paid by the word and can vary. Some magazines and Web sites pay per review. The price per word can be determined by experience. Some writers will take a job for a small sum in the hopes that they will earn more money as they continue to write for and develop a relationship with a particular publication.

Outlook

Music writing is a very competitive field. You should expect the going to be slightly harder than in some of the other jobs we've discussed. As long as people continue to listen to music, others will be there in some capacity to talk about it. If you are not writing for anyone and don't have a portfolio or writing samples, write reviews of records you like or feel strongly about, and send them to various publications. don't always expect to receive replies to your submissions. Be prepared to have your writing rejected sometimes. The more you write, the better your work will be, and the better your chances of being published.

FOR MORE INFORMATION

WEB SITES

Music-critic.com
http://www.music-critic.com
Check out these online reviews of the latest in rock, pop, electronica, urban, jazz, classical, and country releases, and see if you can do better.

MusicJournalist.com
http://www.musicphotographer.com
This site has tips and resources specifically for music writers and photographers. Includes industry directories; news, features, and articles; and mailing lists.

BOOKS

Bangs, Lester. *Psychotic Reactions and Carburetor Dung*. New York: Vintage Books, 1998.
A collection of Lester Bangs's writing from the early 1970s up until his death in 1982.

DeRogatis, Jim. *Let It Blurt*. New York: Broadway Books, 2000.
Let It Blurt is the biography of Lester Bangs, the man who changed the face of music criticism forever. His story is sad, funny, and moving. Just as memorable is the included rare essay entitled "How To Be A Music Critic."

Fong-Torres, Ben, and Cameron Crowe. *Not Fade Away: A Backstage Pass to 20 Years of Rock & Roll*. San Francisco: Backbeat Books, 1999.
This book has interviews with and editorials about musicians from a renowned critic.

Meltzer, Richard. *The Aesthetics of Rock*. New York: De Capo Paperbacks, 1987.
In this book, Meltzer, a music writer, explores the music scene "on the edge" from 1966 to 1968.

PERIODICALS

Mojo
Web site: http://www.mojo4music.com
MOJO is an expensive British magazine but has some of the best writing about music on the planet. Go to a bookstore and leaf through a copy—it's like reading the history of rock, R & B, and rap in every issue.

Pollstar
4697 W. Jacquelyn Avenue
Fresno, CA 93722
(559) 271-7900
Web site: http://www.pollstar.com
A print magazine with an online component, *Pollstar* publishes concert tour schedules for music professionals.

Rolling Stone
Web site: http://www.rollingstone.com
A bimonthly popular culture magazine, *Rolling Stone* covers the entertainment industry with a special focus on music.

Spin
Web site: http://www.spin.com
The print and online versions of this magazine cover everything you'd want to know about the latest in rock music.

Vibe
Web site: http://www.vibe.com
Good music writing about rap and R & B music can be found in *Vibe*.

FOR FUN

Almost Famous (2000)
DreamWorks SKG
A teenager gets his first gig writing about a band and following them on tour in this movie starring Kate Hudson and Billy Crudup.

12

START YOUR OWN RECORD LABEL

If you love music and want to put your own mark on the industry, you may want to think about going into business for yourself! You don't need a million dollars, or even a thousand—only a desire to succeed and the will to work for a really demanding employer: you.

Description

There are usually a few major record labels on the scene at any given time. Who are they? Their products are the ones you'll be most likely to see in larger stores, or hear on the radio, or see on video a few times in any given day. Record labels that may not have as much money to promote their acts or distribute their records are known as independent labels. Many independent labels are small-frys—regular young men and women who love music and are trying to paint their corner of the world with their musical vision.

So you decide to start a label. Great. What now?

First, you need what any young enterprising go-getter requires: money. Not a lot of money, just some money to cover the basic expenses, like pressing the records or CDs your label is putting out. You'll also need to cover the costs of legally owning the name to your label. Regardless of the title—Wreckords, I Love Music Records—you'll want to own the rights to it so no one else can use your brand name to sell their records.

Another important item to consider is who is going to release records on your new label? Well, if you are musically inclined, maybe you could be the first artist on your label. If you don't want to wear too many hats in your new

Indie folk-rock queen Ani DiFranco records on her own label, Righteous Babe Records, which allows her to produce music without interference from studio executives.

line of work, you'll have to seek out talent. You can't sign someone who already has a contract, so you'll have to hunt for people just like yourself: independents. Most musicians who aren't session musicians or who work at their craft part-time will be like you. They aren't expecting a million-dollar signing bonus for agreeing to release their music through you.

So why would someone release their music through you?

Good question. As the head of a label, your job is also to take care of the day-to-day details concerning your

If you want to sign bands to your label, you should attend local shows to discover new talents like Arbor Day (above).

clients. Depending on the size of your company (remember to start small!), the needs will not be incredibly demanding, but they'll still keep you busy and require you to be organized and dedicated.

You'll still need to find clients, though. Do this by asking friends who are in bands or by going to local performances. Legwork pays off. Attending as many local shows and concerts as you can will give you a good idea of the talent pool in your area and will help you determine what kind of music you want to represent your label.

Working online can help those who start their own record label compete with the big leaguers. Close contact with fans and potential fans can be accomplished through a professional Web site and e-mail distribution.

The key to running your own label these days is through your computer. Doing business online can be your best friend. You can e-mail people who have signed your band's mailing list at a show and let them know what the band is doing. This is also a great chance to let them know about any other recordings your label may have to offer or any breaking news such as new signings, or unscheduled or short notice shows. Hopefully, they will pass the word on to their friends. You can also take this a step further and devote a Web site to your label and your clients.

Education and Training

Running your own label is learned through experience. Many people who start their own labels do so after spending some time working in the record industry in some way (usually by interning at a large record label) in order to learn the basics about the business. The fundamental aspects of record labels are incredibly similar, despite the number of clients on your roster, the number of your employees, or the audience you reach.

As mentioned earlier in this book, start small and start soon. Computer experience will make this and many of the professions listed in this book easier. There are employers out there who won't hire people without some sort of computer experience. It makes sense for the head of a record label to know how to navigate through the digital age.

Outlook

There aren't any hard and fast statistics on employment rates for people who follow this line of work. It's safe to say in this case that your input can definitely affect the outcome. As we said earlier, music is ultimately a creative project. Applying the same creativity to any job that involves music will help you make your venture more successful.

FOR MORE INFORMATION

WEB SITES

Ace Fu Records
http://www.acefu.com

My Pal God Records
http://www.mypalgodrecords.com
Ace Fu Records and My Pal God Records are two Web sites that were started by ordinary people with very little money. Both Web sites have a section that tells a little about the difficult process of starting a record label.

DIYsearch
http://www.diysearch.com
This search engine (DIY stands for "do it yourself") is a nonprofit cataloguing resource for independent artists, focusing on the arts, music, and humanities communities.

Independent Record Distribution Network
http://www.pan.com/indie/dist.htm
This is an online resource for distributing audio recordings that have been independently produced and released.

Internet Music Resource Guide
http://www.specialweb.com/music
This is a reference of links and other resources to Internet sites about music.

Soundclick.com
http://www.soundclick.com
This site features signed and unsigned bands. Labels can send MP3s of their artists to the site.

BOOKS

Frascogna Xavier M., and H. Lee Hetherington. *This Business of Artist Management.* New York: Billboard Books, 1997.
This Business of Artist Management will help anyone intending to work with musicians for a living.

Kashif and Gary Greenberg. *Everything You'd Better Know About the Record Industry.* Venice, CA: Brooklyn Boy Books, 1996.
This is a comprehensive guide for anyone who wants to pursue a career in the music industry. Rapper Ice Cube calls it the new bible for the recording industry.

Krasilovsky, M. William, Sidney Shemel, and John Gross. *This Business of Music: The Definitive Guide to the Music Industry*. New York: Watson-Guptill Publishers, 2000.
This is a comprehensive reference to the economic, legal, and financial aspects of the music business. It's known as the definitive book on the music industry.

Lathrop, Tad, and Jim Pettigrew. *This Business of Music Marketing and Promotion*. New York: Billboard Books, 1999.
This is a guide to planning and producing a complete marketing campaign for selling music to the listening public.

Passman, Donald S. *All You Need to Know About the Music Business*. New York: Simon and Schuster, 2000.
This book gives advice about negotiating deals, advisers, publishing, touring, and merchandising. It includes helpful information for anyone interested in pursuing a career in the music industry.

Schulenberg, Richard. *Legal Aspects of the Record Industry: An Insider's View*. New York: Billboard Books, 1999.
This is an overview of all things legal with regards to the music industry. It includes annotated examples of contracts.

Schwartz, Daylle Deanna. *Start and Run Your Own Record Label*. New York: Billboard Books, 1998.
This book is especially useful for beginners. Quotes from industry professionals will help those who need to know all aspects of the music business.

Sweeney, Tim, and Mark Geller. *Tim Sweeney's Guide to Releasing Independent Records*. Torrance, CA: T.S.A. Books, 1996.
This book teaches the reader how to set up his or her own independent label, produce records, get distribution into major retail outlets, design a promotional strategy, and get records played.

GLOSSARY

book To schedule a band or an artist to play live music in a venue.

clips Published writing samples.

commission A percentage of the profit earned by a performance, an artist, or a recording.

distro Short for "distribution."

DIY Do it yourself.

feedback The high-pitched output that often occurs when someone speaks into a microphone.

format The type of music a radio station plays.

free-form A radio station that plays music across all genres and doesn't stick to one format.

guerrilla promotions A local, grassroots form of promotion involving street teams.

indie Shorthand for independent; in the music business, it refers to performers or labels who are "small" and don't have a large amount of financial support.

mixing board or **mixer** Equipment used by a DJ or a sound engineer that combines and adjusts sounds from different sources.

mom and pop Term used to describe labels and music stores that are run by a few individuals, rather than by a large conglomerate.

music notation The written language of music.

playlist A list of songs that the music director of a radio station has determined will be played by the station's disc jockeys.

portfolio A collection of an applicant's work (usually writing samples or art pieces) that serves as a sort of résumé.

promo Short for "promotional." Promos are usually free CDs given to writers, distributors, and music stores to promote a piece of music that is scheduled for an upcoming release.

repertoire The group of songs that a singer or a musician is prepared to perform.

residency A regular, long-term gig for a band or DJ to perform in a venue.

roadie Also known as instrument technician. Prepares the set for a musician, a band, or a show by tuning the instruments, checking the sound, and doing other tasks that contribute to the success of a production.

street team A group of unpaid people hired by a record company to promote a musician or a band at the street level.

INDEX

About the Author

Kerry Hinton is a freelance writer who lives in Hoboken, New Jersey. He has spent the past six years working in and writing about the music industry. He currently manages a record store.

Photo Credits

Cover © FPG International; pp. 9, 10 © Willie Hill Jr./The Image Works; p. 12 © Tomas del Amo/Index Stock Imagery; p. 13 © Grantpix/Index Stock Imagery; pp. 21, 22 © S.I.N/Corbis; p. 26 © Arlean Collins/The Image Works; pp. 32, 34 © James Keyser/TimePix; p. 37 © Tony Dejak/AP Wide World Photos; pp. 43, 50 © Ghislain and Marie David de Lossy/The Image Bank; p. 44 © Jacques M. Cherret/Corbis; p. 46 © Mark Humphrey/AP Wide World Photos; p. 49 © Syracuse Newspapers/The Image Works; pp. 56, 58 © Tom Sistak/*The (Ottawa) Daily Times*/AP Wide World Photos; p. 59 © Bill Varie/Corbis; p. 60 © SuperStock; pp. 67, 69 © Larry Lawfer/Index Stock Imagery; p. 72 © Grantpix/Index Stock Imagery, Inc.; pp. 77, 78 © Tina Fineberg/AP Wide World Photos; p. 80 © Michael S. Yamashita/Corbis; pp. 85, 86 © Bob Daemmrich/The Image Works; p. 88 © Reuters NewMedia Inc./Corbis; pp. 95 and 96 by Cindy Reiman; p. 99 © Ed Bailey/AP Wide World Photos; pp. 105, 106 © Gianni Cigolini/The Image

Bank; p. 109 © Michael Siluk/The Image Works; pp. 116, 120 © Lynn Goldsmith/Corbis; p. 118 © The Everett Collection; pp. 124, 126 © Jim Barcus/AP Wide World Photos; p. 127 by Tahara Hasan; p. 128 © Vicky Kasala/The Image Bank.

Design and Layout

Evelyn Horovicz